Where Yellowstone?

by Sarah Fabiny

illustrated by Stephen Marchesi

Penguin Workshop

For all those who work to preserve and protect
Yellowstone National Park—SF

To Janet, for her patience and friendship
these many years—SM

PENGUIN WORKSHOP
An imprint of Penguin Random House LLC, New York

First published in the United States of America by Penguin Workshop,
an imprint of Penguin Random House LLC, New York, 2024

Visit us online at penguinrandomhouse.com.

Library of Congress Cataloging-in-Publication Data is available.

Printed in the United States of America

ISBN 9780593660881 (paperback)   10 9 8 7 6 5 4 3 2 1 CJKW
ISBN 9780593660898 (library binding)   10 9 8 7 6 5 4 3 2 1 CJKW

Contents

Where Is Yellowstone?

In 2022, Yellowstone National Park celebrated its 150th birthday. Most birthdays are celebrated on just one day of the year, marking the actual date that someone was born. But that's not the case when you're the first national park in the United States—and the world!

When you're Yellowstone National Park, covering 3,472 square miles (that's larger than Rhode Island and Delaware combined), your birthday celebration lasts for six months. There's a lot to celebrate!

Unfortunately, due to the COVID-19 pandemic,

the party wasn't able to be as big as originally planned. There were no large in-person events, but there were some small ones at the park and lots of online festivities. The celebrations, which lasted from March to September 2022, included educational programs, a brand-new Tribal Heritage Center, free Junior Ranger programs, and a conference about the park's future.

Even though Yellowstone's birthday is marked as 1872, its history actually begins far before that date. And this area of the country wasn't as untouched as most people think. For thousands of years, native people lived in and traveled through the region. And park officials made sure these people were honored at the birthday celebrations.

Yellowstone National Park's creation led to many more national parks opening in the United States. Sequoia and Yosemite National Parks opened in 1890, and Mount Rainier was added in 1899. Today, there are sixty-three national parks, with the newest being New River Gorge in West Virginia, which was added in December 2020.

Thanks to Yellowstone National Park, the United States is now full of exciting national parks for people of all ages to explore. That's certainly something worth celebrating—even when the birthday party is over!

CHAPTER 1
Old and New

Yellowstone has been a national park for over 150 years, which might sound like a long time. But the amazing mountains, valleys, geysers, and waterfalls in the park were created by forces of nature millions of years ago.

The outer layer of the earth is made up of large areas called tectonic plates. These plates, which are miles and miles thick, are always moving— but at a very slow pace. As the plates slowly shift, they come together, drift apart, or slide past each other. All this movement creates mountains and valleys and causes earthquakes and volcanic activity.

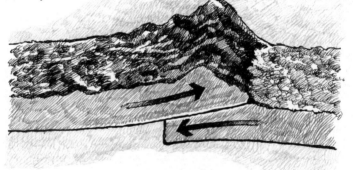

Tectonic plates

Most of the mountains, valleys, earthquakes, and volcanoes across the world occur where two plates meet. But Yellowstone is located right in the middle of one of the tectonic plates—the North American Plate. Also in the middle of this plate is a huge mass of molten rock, or lava. Some of this lava has made (or oozed) its way to the earth's surface over the past millions of years. As it has flowed across the landscape, it has created the natural wonders in Yellowstone.

The landscape of the Yellowstone region began forming about 150 million years ago. Many of the landforms in the park, mainly the mountains, were created around the beginning of the Cenozoic (say: see-nuh-ZOW-uhk) Era. (The Cenozoic Era, which means "recent life," began 66 million years ago, and it is the period the earth is still in today.) Then about 30 million years ago, the area around Yellowstone began stretching. The canyons and basins seen in the park were formed during this time. (A basin is like a bowl in the earth's surface. It is a depression, or dip, with raised sides.) And about 16.5 million years ago, a period of extreme volcanic activity took place.

Yellowstone's Biscuit Basin

Possible Prehistoric Park Residents

Even though no humans were around to watch the formation of the mountains, valleys, geysers, and waterfalls in the Yellowstone area, there may have been some park residents who witnessed this—dinosaurs. Scientists recently announced that a fossil discovered in the park in 1966 is the tooth of a young *Tyrannosaurus rex*.

Allosaurus

Thanks to this discovery, *T. rex* can claim to be the first identifiable dinosaur fossil to have been found within Yellowstone National Park. Fossils from other dinosaur species, including *Allosaurus* and *Diplodocus*, have been found in the area outside the park. Just over three hours away from Yellowstone is the Wyoming Dinosaur Center. It is home to one of the largest and most unique dinosaur fossil collections in the world.

The first major eruption in Yellowstone took place about 2.1 million years ago. It is believed to be one of the largest volcanic eruptions ever to take place on our planet. The ash that was spewed out by the volcano covered a massive area. It dumped ash as far away as present-day Missouri, which is over 1,000 miles away. Scientists have found that other major eruptions occurred 1.3 million and 640,000 years ago.

Each time there was a volcanic eruption, the amount of magma under the surface was reduced. (Magma is molten rock when it is underground, and lava is molten rock that breaks through the earth's surface). When the amount of magma was reduced in the eruptions, it left a caldera. (A caldera is a large volcanic crater). The volcanic eruption that took place 640,000 years ago formed a caldera that is about fifty-two by twenty-eight miles wide. Even with all these volcanic eruptions, there is still magma underneath the surface in the Yellowstone region.

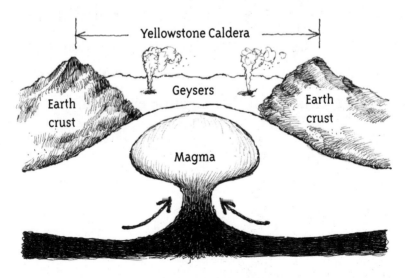

What's really amazing is that Yellowstone National Park doesn't just have volcanoes—it *is* an active volcano. Not only is it an active volcano, but it is also a supervolcano. This means that it has had a huge eruption on a scale that geologists use to measure volcanic eruptions called the Volcanic Explosivity Index. This scale, which goes from zero to eight, is similar to the Richter scale, which is used to measure earthquakes. And the eruption that occurred in the Yellowstone area 2.1 million years ago is at the very top of this scale.

So, what are the chances of this supervolcano erupting in the future? Scientists say that it is possible, but it's far more likely that Yellowstone will never have another gigantic eruption.

Geysers and hot springs are evidence
of the Yellowstone supervolcano

CHAPTER 2
First Settlers

Once the ice melted after the most recent Ice Age, about 11,500–14,000 years ago, the Yellowstone region became home to all kinds of plants and animals. As the area got warmer and drier, native people followed. And for thousands

of years before Yellowstone became a national park, it was a place where these native people hunted, fished, gathered plants, and used the hot springs for religious and healing purposes.

Archaeologists used to believe that ancient people could not have lived in an area that was at such a high elevation because of the harsh climate in the winter. (An archaeologist is someone who studies the things that people made, used, and left behind in ancient times.) But when artifacts such as stone tools and spear points were found in the park in the 1870s, scientists changed their opinion.

Scientists believe the native people used these stone tools and spear points for hunting bison, mountain sheep, and deer that roamed the area during that time. It is believed that they also gathered nuts, seeds, and fruit that grew in the region. And scientists have found hand-crafted bowls made from soapstone that were most likely used for storage and cooking. (Soapstone is a soft rock that can be carved into shapes.)

As time passed, the climate in Yellowstone changed. It has varied between warm and dry and cool and wet over the past ten thousand years. Many plants adapted to these changing conditions. The people in the area also adapted to the changing climate, and they continued to hunt the animals and gather plants that lived in the area. Scientists have actually found campsites and trails that were used by these native people thousands of years ago. In fact, some of the trails used in the park today were probably used by native people.

About three thousand years ago, more native
people moved into the area and used it as a
source of food, fuel, and building materials.
During this time native people also began to use

bows and arrows for hunting. They also used traps to capture animals, and it's believed they built corrals—fenced-in areas—in which to keep bison.

The Tukudika

Many tribes spent time in the Yellowstone area, but most left when winter arrived. However, members of one tribe, the Tukudika, stayed through the season. They are believed to be the earliest known permanent residents of what is now Yellowstone National Park. Tukudika means "eaters of the mountain sheep," and the tribe was given the name because bighorn sheep were their main source of meat.

The tribe stayed at lower elevations in the winter months to avoid the worst of the deep snow and cold temperatures. But in the warmer months they traveled up into the mountains, following the sheep. Since it was difficult for horses to make their way up the rocky landscape, the Tukudika used dogs to carry their packs as they hunted. The dogs weren't just used for carrying things—they were sheep hunters, too!

Tukudika people, 1871

The Tukudika lived in the Yellowstone area for thousands of years. But once the national park was established, they were moved to reservations in what is now Wyoming and Idaho. (A reservation is an area of land set aside by the US government for Native Americans where they can govern themselves and maintain their traditions.) Today, some descendants of the Tukudika still live on these reservations.

Native people came to know the Yellowstone region very well. So when explorers and trappers who had sailed to North America began to make their way into the area, native people often acted as guides. Native people who lived in what is

now North Dakota told the Lewis and Clark Expedition to follow a road that traveled to the source of the Yellowstone River. A group of native people guided a man named Warren Angus Ferris to the geysers along the Firehole River.

Warren Angus Ferris, as well as other explorers and trappers, reported that the native people were afraid of the hot springs and geysers in the area. They claimed that the tribes believed that evil spirits came from the thermal waters—but that wasn't the truth. Even though it was false, explorers and settlers continued to pass on this lie that the indigenous people were frightened by the geysers and hot springs in the region. Soon it became the story that was told about the area's native people.

According to some native people, the spirits were actually kind and helpful. And if you approached the geysers and hot springs in a humble and gentle way, the power of these spirits could be harnessed. There is evidence that native people used hot springs for cooking food and bathed in the water for healing purposes. On occasion, they also buried their dead in the bubbling water instead of burying them in the dirt.

When the park was established in the late nineteenth century, the US government wanted the area to be seen as wilderness. The government didn't want visitors to know that native people had been living in Yellowstone for a long time. The government was worried that the presence of native tribes in the park might scare some tourists and keep them from visiting. So, the lies about the tribes being afraid of the geysers and hot springs were repeated. The government used that false information as an excuse to move the native people off the land. The public was falsely told that native people had never lived in Yellowstone.

Within the past few decades, Yellowstone National Park and the US government have been working to tell the true story of how native people were and still are connected to the area.

They want people to know that native people have lived in the area for thousands of years but were forced to move out of the park when it was established in 1872. It is important that the history of the region include the history of the native tribes, the original humans to love and take care of the land.

CHAPTER 3
Land of Wonder

By the 1700s, French fur trappers and traders had made their way to the remote Yellowstone area. On a map from 1797, a river in the area was labeled *R. des roches Jaune*, (which means "River of the Yellow Rock" in French).

In English, the river, as well as the territory that surrounded it, became known as "Yellow Stone." The trappers and traders saw the breathtaking geysers, waterfalls, and mountains as they hunted beavers. And they told stories of the amazing and unique landscape to anyone who would listen.

In 1827, a Philadelphia newspaper printed a letter from a trapper who described "hot and boiling springs" and "an explosion . . . resembling that of thunder." But most people who heard or read these descriptions thought they were just made up! How could a place like this exist? In 1869, three mine workers who lived in the Montana Territory, David Folsom, Charles Cook, and William Peterson, set off on the first unofficial exploration expedition of the area. They had originally planned to be part of an expedition that was to have a military escort. But when the military escort fell through, the other members of the party decided not to go.

David Folsom, Charles Cook, and William Peterson

However, Folsom, Cook, and Peterson decided to make the difficult and dangerous journey on their own. Cook and Folsom kept journals as the men made their way across the wilderness. When they returned, Cook sent an account of their expedition to a magazine. The response he received said, "Thank you but we do not publish fiction." The magazine thought he had made everything up! It was still too hard for people to believe that a place filled with steaming, hissing landforms was real. But it was the members of this expedition who first came up with the idea of preserving and protecting this landscape as a national park.

In 1862, Nathaniel Langford moved to the Montana Territory in search of gold. Shortly

Nathaniel Langford

after his arrival, he began hearing stories about the land that lay to the south. Hunters, trappers, and mountain men who had lived and worked in the area talked about places with names like Hot Spring Brimstone, Devil's Slide, and Burnt Hole. Nathaniel had yet to find any gold, and he thought perhaps this region with the strange names might be a good place to look. Backed by Jay Cooke, one of the country's wealthiest men, Nathaniel organized an expedition. Cooke owned a railroad, and he was hoping that the expedition could convince the US government that another railway line should be built across the United States—cutting right through the Yellowstone region.

Nathaniel Langford had trouble finding people to join him. But he finally put together a team of nineteen other men that included some soldiers, a lawyer, and a newspaper reporter. None of these men, including Langford, had any experience trekking in the mountains. Fortunately, Henry Washburn, a former general in the Civil War agreed to lead the group. He could provide leadership as well as survival skills.

Henry Washburn

The expedition set out in August 1870, and it lasted for about six weeks. During that time the men attempted to measure and analyze some of the landforms they encountered, all the while taking notes about the incredible things they saw. But an early snowstorm and a lack of supplies meant the men had to end the expedition sooner than they had planned. When the group returned, Nathaniel Langford wrote articles for newspapers and went on a lecture tour.

Finally, people were interested in hearing more about this wild part of the continent. They began to believe that the tall tales were real. Fortunately, they weren't interested in building another railroad. During one of Nathaniel Langford's lectures in Washington, DC, a man named Ferdinand V. Hayden was in the audience. He was one of the country's leading geologists, and he was listening with excitement.

Ferdinand V. Hayden

Hayden had led expeditions to the West before, so he was familiar with the incredible landscapes there. He had trekked across parts of present-day North Dakota, South Dakota, Wyoming, Montana, and Kansas. On these trips, he gathered rocks and fossils, as well as specimens of plants, insects, and animals. (The Sioux called him "the Man Who Picks Up Stones Running.") But Ferdinand V. Hayden had never traveled to the Yellowstone region before. He was determined to explore that part of the continent. And he was going to get the US Congress to pay for the expedition. (Congress is the branch of government that makes laws and controls spending.) Congress granted him $40,000 (that would be almost one million dollars today) to explore the greater Yellowstone region, and his team set off in June 1871. The group of thirty-four men included guides, cooks, doctors, mapmakers, a zoologist (someone who studies animals), an ornithologist (someone who studies birds), a photographer, and two artists.

A Painter and a Photographer

Ferdinand V. Hayden realized that many people didn't believe the stories about the Yellowstone region because they couldn't picture the landscape. What better way to convince the public about the amazing place than to have a painter and a photographer as part of his team?

Thomas Moran was an American artist who specialized in landscapes. On the expedition, Moran filled a portfolio with sketches and small watercolor paintings of all the amazing waterfalls, canyons, and geysers the team saw. When he returned home, he completed a seven-foot-by-twelve-foot painting entitled *Grand Canyon of the Yellowstone.*

Thomas Moran

The painting was displayed at Congress so people could finally see this spectacular landscape. They no longer had to imagine it.

Along with Thomas Moran, photographer William Henry Jackson was on the expedition. The photography equipment he brought weighed more than three hundred pounds. The glass plates, jugs of water, and containers of chemicals

William Henry Jackson

were carried by his mule, Hypo. Jackson climbed trees, lowered himself into canyons, and reached over waterfalls to capture the breathtaking scenery. He often asked Thomas Moran to pose in a photo so that people would appreciate the scale of what they were seeing. His photos from the expedition caused a sensation and proved that the hot springs, geysers, and waterfalls in the area were very real.

For four months, Hayden and his men made their way across the area, making detailed notes, taking measurements, and collecting samples. They endured harsh weather, freezing temperatures, and even an earthquake. But that didn't stop them from making the most of their time in what Hayden kindly called an "ideal open-air laboratory."

On October 2, Ferdinand V. Hayden officially

ended the survey, which he declared a success. He then spent the next couple of months writing a five-hundred-page report that would be presented to Congress. The report contained detailed notes on their findings and included photos, sketches, and paintings. Hayden also sent the forty-five boxes of specimens they collected to the Smithsonian Institution. (Located in Washington, DC, the Smithsonian Institution is the world's largest museum, education, and research facility. Its collection contains millions of objects.)

The Smithsonian Institution

Hayden wanted to speak to anyone who could help preserve this area of the country. More than anything he wanted Congress to designate the area as a national park. That way, no one could own the land, strip it of its natural resources, or build on it. It would be safe and kept just as it was. Two senators, one from Kansas and one from Illinois, were eager to support Hayden and his idea. They also believed that this wonderland should be preserved and protected, rather than settled and developed.

Union soldiers from the Civil War

Some members of the government also had another reason for wanting to establish a beautiful national park. The country had recently lived through the harsh and bloody Civil War. After the destruction of the war, creating a park would hopefully give the nation a feeling of unity and victory.

So on December 18, 1871, a bill was introduced in Congress to establish a park in the Yellowstone region. It was to be an area of land fifty-five by sixty-five miles, set "apart as a great national park or pleasure-ground for the benefit and enjoyment of the people." The bill was approved by Congress, and on March 1, 1872, President Ulysses Grant signed the Yellowstone National Park Protection Act into law. The United States had its first national park!

Ulysses Grant

CHAPTER 4
Welcome to Yellowstone

The United States had its first national park, and now it needed someone to be in charge of it. In May 1872, the Department of the Interior appointed Nathaniel Langford, who had been part of the 1870 expedition, as the first superintendent of the park. However, he had no staff or budget, was not being paid for his work,

and had another job at the time. Langford did what he could, but it wasn't much.

In 1877, Philetus Norris was appointed as the park's second superintendent. Congress also allocated money "to protect, preserve, and improve the Park." Norris took those words very seriously. During his time on the job, he built roads, fought to get rid of vandals and hunters in the park, and built a park headquarters. However, he also kept sharing the false idea that native tribes feared the area because of the hot springs and geysers. He thought this would help attract visitors to the park.

Philetus Norris

Norris left the post in 1882. For the next four years the park was managed by people who really didn't look after it. So in August 1886, the US Army took charge of Yellowstone. The army guarded the major attractions, patrolled the park's millions of acres, and kicked out troublemakers until 1918. The National Park Service had been created by President Woodrow Wilson in 1916 and took over management of the park after the army. Yellowstone National Park has been managed by the Park Service ever since.

The US Army in Yellowstone

When the park first opened in 1872, fewer than one thousand visitors came that year. It was difficult to get to the park and there weren't many places to stay once people got there. Visitors made the journey on horseback, in horse-drawn carriages or stagecoaches, or even on bicycles. They usually slept in tents. The first railroad to the park was built in 1908, so visitors were able

to access the park by train. And once passenger train service started, the number of tourists greatly increased. In 1908, more than seven thousand people visited the park. Several hotels were built so that visitors could sleep in a comfortable bed and eat in a dining room rather than sleep outside and cook over a campfire.

The Old Faithful Inn

One of the grandest hotels in Yellowstone is the
Old Faithful Inn. It is the largest log structure in the
world. Built from 1903 to 1904, it was designed to
fit into the landscape of the park and used local

stone and lumber in the construction. The lobby is six stories tall and the centerpiece is a huge stone fireplace. When the hotel opened, it boasted about having electric lights and steam heat, which were still quite new at the time. Evening meals were accompanied by a string quartet and there was dancing six nights a week. Meals were served family style at long tables, and dinner cost about seventy-five cents.

The hotel has been expanded and modified since it opened. It currently has over three hundred guest rooms, and there is an observation deck where guests can sit and watch Old Faithful erupt. In 1987, the Old Faithful Inn was declared a National Historic Landmark.

Park managers had resisted letting cars into the park. They felt that vehicles would ruin the landscape. However, in 1915, the first privately owned car officially entered the park. Drivers had to have spare tires and tools with them in their cars to enter. The roads in the park weren't fully paved and many cars got stuck or broke down. But that didn't stop people who had cars from visiting Yellowstone. Just five years later,

over five thousand cars entered the park during the summer season. More hotels and inns were built to accommodate the guests, and more roads were paved to make traveling through the park easier and safer.

In the early days of the park, there were no boardwalks, fences, or off-limits areas. Tourists were able to walk up to hot springs and geysers and get as close to the wildlife as they dared.

Visitors often dropped soap into geysers to try and get them to erupt. Many wanted to take home a souvenir of the park and broke off pieces of rock from the landforms. Bears were often chained to trees and elk were put into cages so that tourists could see them up close. It was not good for the animals that called this place home.

People began to worry that the nation's first national park was becoming an amusement park. There were calls to make sure that this amazing ecosystem was being protected. (An ecosystem is a community of living organisms and non-living things that interact in an area.) The National Park Service wanted to make sure every tourist had a fun, enjoyable, and safe trip to the park. But they also wanted to ensure that the natural features and the plants and wildlife were being looked after. Boardwalks were built and certain areas were declared off-limits.

More scientific research took place, and education programs were started to teach tourists about the wonders of the park.

After World War II, park attendance skyrocketed. In 1948, more than one million people visited the park for the first time ever. And that number doubled by 1965. Now more than ever, the National Park Service had to find a balance between making the park a tourist attraction and a place for protection and preservation.

In the 1970s, people pushed to have the park focus on conservation. Hiking, boating, fishing, and swimming were restricted. In 1976, the park was declared a biosphere reserve. And in 1978, it was designated as a World Heritage Site by the United Nations. The world recognized that this unique ecosystem must be protected and preserved for generations to come. Even though the park has put many rules and regulations in place, it is still one of the most visited spots on the planet. Today, around four million tourists from around the world make their way to Yellowstone every year.

(Don't) Feed the Bears

As more people came to visit the park, the more garbage they created. The hotels had garbage dumps, and pretty soon the bears began hanging around them. They were an easy source of food for the bears. At first this was seen as a nuisance, but soon it became a tourist attraction. Garbage was purposely dumped in areas so that tourists could watch the furry residents of the park up close. Bears then started showing up along the roads, knowing that visitors would stop and throw food to them. Tourists were warned that the bears were wild, not tame. But people would hold food out in their hands, and more than one visitor ended up with a scratch or a bite. And the bears caused damage to cars and fences as they were looking for handouts.

It wasn't until the 1960s that the National Park

Service started phasing out bear feeding in the
park. They recognized it was having a bad impact
on the bears and posed a threat to tourists. In
1970, the practice was officially banned in the
park. Since then, the park has worked to educate
visitors about keeping a safe distance from wildlife
in the park and respecting the animals' habitat.

CHAPTER 5
Geysers Galore

The indigenous people who lived and traveled through the Yellowstone region were familiar with the hydrothermal features in the area. (A hydrothermal feature involves water that has been heated in the earth's crust.) They gave those places names that referred to these hydrothermal features.

Hot spring

To the Crow, it was the "land of the burning ground"; to the Blackfeet it was known as "many smoke"; to the Flathead it was "smoke from the ground"; and the Kiowa called it "the place of hot water." They considered these features sacred.

Scientists had known about geysers for some time before the Yellowstone expeditions. However, most of those hydrothermal features were located in Iceland. (The English word *geyser* comes from the Icelandic word *Geysir*, the name of a hot spring in southwest Iceland.) But when trappers and explorers came upon the hydrothermal features in the Yellowstone region, they almost didn't understand what they were seeing. Many early explorers feared these hot and often stinky explosions of water were a sign of the devil. By the time the Hayden expedition made its way through the area, the team realized they had come across something unique. They had come upon the largest

Travertine terraces

collection of hydrothermal features in the world.

The hydrothermal feature that Yellowstone is best known for is its geysers. When geysers erupt, they release a mix of water and steam. In order to keep erupting, a geyser needs a supply of water and a constant source of heat. Which means that most geysers are found in areas that get lots of rain or snow and also have volcanic activity.

The rain and snow give a supply of water, and the volcanic activity beneath the earth's surface heats that water. Quite often geysers are found in groups called geyser fields.

Castle Geyser

Yellowstone Hot Spots

The park has five different types of hydrothermal features:

Hot Springs—pools containing water that has been heated by magma in the earth's crust

Geysers—hot springs that erupt

Mudpots—pools containing hot, bubbling mud

Travertine Terraces—platforms of limestone rock formed by water that contains minerals

Fumaroles—holes or vents that release steam into the air

Mudpots

Beehive Geyser

Geysers are actually quite rare, and most of the world's geysers are in just five countries: the United States, Iceland, Russia, New Zealand, and Chile. There are only about one thousand geysers around the world—and half of those are in Yellowstone National Park.

Geysers need underground cavities where the water, steam, and pressure can collect. What turns a hot spring into a geyser is a "problem with the plumbing," usually near the surface. With a hot spring, the heated water just gurgles to the surface. With a geyser, the problem is that there is a tight squeeze in the underground rock. The water can't easily get from the underground cavity to the surface. Because of that, pressure builds up. And when the pressure and temperature are just right, an eruption occurs. The eruption stops when there is no more water in the underground cavity or when the rock around the cavity has cooled down.

Many geysers around the world are used as energy sources. However, many of the geyser fields in the world have been disrupted because of energy development. Practically all of New Zealand's geysers are "dead" because they have been tapped as an energy resource. Because of this, Yellowstone's sources of heat and hot water are not used for human purposes. The goal is to keep the hydrothermal features in Yellowstone erupting, bubbling, and steaming for centuries to come, so humans are encouraged not to interfere with them.

Old Faithful

The most famous geyser in Yellowstone, and the most famous geyser in the world, is Old Faithful.

Watching Old Faithful erupt is a Yellowstone tradition. People from all over the world come to watch this geyser erupt on its predictable schedule.

There are no records of what native people thought of Old Faithful. In 1870, the Washburn-Langford-Doane expedition documented their sighting of the geyser. Langford gave the geyser its name because it erupted so often and the eruptions were predictable.

Since 1870, more than one million eruptions at Old Faithful have been recorded. Eruptions occur about twenty times a day (about every ninety minutes) and last for about one and a half to five minutes. The water can blast about 90 to 180 feet into the air, and the water temperature has been measured to be around 204 degrees Fahrenheit. (Water boils at 212 degrees Fahrenheit.)

CHAPTER 6
A World of Wildlife

The wildlife in Yellowstone National Park is just about as famous as its geysers. There are around three hundred species of birds, sixty-seven species of mammals, sixteen species of fish, six species of reptiles, and five species of amphibians.

Great gray owl

The park is also home to the largest concentration of mammals in the lower forty-eight states.

The species of birds in the park include everything from soaring eagles and quacking ducks, to chirping songbirds and hooting owls. So many birds call the park home because it provides so many different types of habitats. The birds can build nests in dense forests and grassy prairies or along rushing rivers and bubbling hot springs. For many of the birds, Yellowstone is just a stop along the way as they migrate across North America. The park gets very cold and snowy in the winter, so most birds are unable to live there all year round.

Mountain chickadee

The mammals in Yellowstone National Park can be seen burrowing underground, climbing trees, galloping across fields, building dams,

Deer mouse

diving for fish—as well as many other kinds of activities. As with the birds, the park provides a variety of habitats to support so many varieties of mammals. The animals range in size from the tiny deer mouse to the majestic bison.

Bison are one of the great symbols of Yellowstone, and you can spot them in many areas of the park. In any one year, the park is home to about six thousand bison. Although the bison, who graze on grass and similar plants, look calm, they are actually the most dangerous animals in the park. More visitors have been injured by bison than any other animal, including grizzly bears.

Bison or Buffalo?

The bison in Yellowstone National Park are often (mistakenly) called buffalo. However, bison and buffalo are not the same. They are two different animals. They don't look like each other, and they don't live on the same continents.

Bison

Bison are native to Europe and North America, and buffalo are native to Asia and Africa. Bison have larger heads and humps, and buffalo have longer and curvier horns. Yellowstone is the only place in the United States where bison have lived continuously since prehistoric times.

Buffalo

Elk

Elk are the most abundant mammal found in Yellowstone National Park. It's estimated that in the summer about ten thousand to twenty thousand elk make their home in the park. The elk eat and graze on lots of plant life in the park, from grasses and shrubs to tree bark, pine tree needles, and aquatic plants. The elk are also an important food source for many other animals in the park, including bears, wolves, mountain lions, coyotes, and birds that scavenge for food.

Because the elk eat so many different kinds of plants and are an important food source for so many other animals, the elk population has an impact on the entire ecosystem.

Since the last glaciers melted in the area after the last Ice Age, fish have lived in the lakes and rivers in the Yellowstone region. And for thousands of years, humans have harvested the fish for food. The native species include cutthroat trout, mountain whitefish, and longnose sucker.

Yellowstone cutthroat trout

While hunting is prohibited in the park, there is a fishing season in Yellowstone and it attracts a lot of tourists who love to fish. When the park first opened, several non-native species of fish were added into the lakes and rivers. But soon these fish started to take over in the park's waters. By the 1930s, managers realized how dangerous the non-native species were to the ecosystem. The Park Service then stopped stocking non-native fish in the lakes and rivers so that the number of native fish would grow.

Yellowstone National Park is home to only six species of reptiles. That's because of the cool, dry conditions in the park. Reptiles prefer habitats that are damp and warm and get lots of sunlight. Of the six species of reptiles, five of them are snakes. The sixth species is the sagebrush lizard, and it is the only type of lizard to live in the

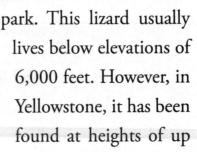

park. This lizard usually lives below elevations of 6,000 feet. However, in Yellowstone, it has been found at heights of up

Sagebrush lizard

to 8,300 feet above sea level. During the mating season, male sagebrush lizards will do push-ups to display the bright blue patches on their sides to ward off other males. These lizards can also shed their tails when grabbed or threatened.

The five species of amphibians in the park include two species of frogs, two species of toads, and one species of salamander. To survive winter in Yellowstone, some of these species go into water that does not freeze, and others move to underground burrows. One species of frog, the boreal chorus frog, can actually survive freezing temperatures. The frogs have special proteins in their system that act like antifreeze. Amphibians are

Boreal chorus frog

very sensitive to pollution, drought, disease, and changes in the amount of precipitation. Because of this, the number of amphibians in the park provides valuable information on environmental changes in the area.

And let's not forget about all the plant life in Yellowstone National Park! Around 1,300 types of plants can be found there, including hundreds of kinds of wildflowers, as well as many species of shrubs, trees, and grasses. The plant life in Yellowstone is much like the plant life in the Rocky Mountain and Great Plains regions that surround the park. However, there

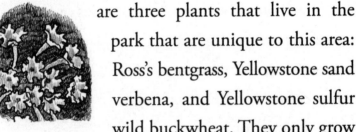

are three plants that live in the park that are unique to this area: Ross's bentgrass, Yellowstone sand verbena, and Yellowstone sulfur wild buckwheat. They only grow in the park and nowhere else.

Yellowstone sand verbena

That's because they can withstand the hot temperatures and mineral-rich water found near the hydrothermal features. People wanting to see the park's rarest plant species, the

Yellowstone sand verbena, are sworn to secrecy. The plant's location is closely guarded and those who are lucky enough to see it are told they cannot tell anyone else where the plant grows. That's because park rangers are worried that people might pick or trample the plant, which could lead to its extinction.

When Yellowstone National Park was established in 1872, it was to be a "public park or pleasuring-ground for the benefit and enjoyment of the people." It is still that. However, the world now understands that the amazing plants and animals that live there need to be preserved and protected as well.

Gray Wolf Project

The world has come to understand how important Yellowstone is as an ecosystem. However, that wasn't always the case. In the 1920s, all the gray wolf packs that lived in the park were killed. They were seen as a threat to tourists, as well as to livestock that lived in the region. But with no wolves in the park, the elk population boomed. And soon all those elk were eating more vegetation than ever before. The grasslands and the forest were being destroyed. The food chain had been upset.

Scientists realized that all the wildlife in the park's ecosystem act like a well-oiled machine. Changing one thing had an impact on everything. So, in January 1995, fourteen gray wolves were brought to the park. Today, there are over one hundred gray wolves living in Yellowstone. And the elk are no longer overgrazing, and the ecosystem has become more balanced.

CHAPTER 7
A Trip to Yellowstone

Since Yellowstone National Park opened in 1872, approximately two hundred million people have visited. Today, about 83 percent of the visitors are from the United States, and 17 percent come from other countries. In 2021, the months of May, June, July, August, and September were the busiest on record. And July 2021 was the busiest month in Yellowstone's history. It was also the first time over a million visitors came to the park in a single month.

Maybe you have already visited Yellowstone and seen all the incredible sights and made memories for a lifetime. If you haven't had the chance to visit our country's first national park, have you ever thought about what a trip there would be like?

Yellowstone visitors, July 2021

What do you think you'd see and do? If you

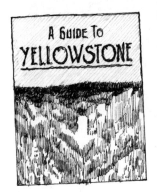

do plan a trip, here are some things to keep in mind!

Because the park is so big, there are five entrances: West, North, Northeast, East, and South. Which entrance you use will make it easier to see and do certain things. The West Entrance is the most popular, as it is the entrance closest to the fantastic hot springs and geysers. Backpackers and mountain lovers often use the South Entrance as this area of the park is remote mountain country and provides great hiking experiences.

South Entrance

To see all of the top sights in the park, you will need at least three days. Because of the park's gigantic size, you will probably spend a few hours each day driving from sight to sight. And you may stop to take in the landscape, slow down to deal with an animal traffic jam, or circle a parking lot looking for an empty space since there are so many visitors.

There are so many things to see and do in the
park that it might be worth taking a guided tour.
These tours can guarantee that you see the sights
you are most excited about. The tours can be done
on foot or in a vehicle. There are also tours if you
want to experience the park in a special way. For
instance, there are tours for people who want to
paint, photograph, or fish in the park.

One of the most fun ways to see the park is on a bicycle! Being on a bike means you get to see more of the sights that are off the main roads. But if you're on a bike, make sure you keep your eyes open for the park's wildlife, as you don't want to startle them.

There are plenty of lakes, rivers, streams, and hot springs in Yellowstone, but as of 2023, there is only one designated spot to swim in the park. That's mainly because the hot springs are *very* hot and the mountain rivers can be *very* cold, plus many of them have dangerous currents.

And where do you want to stay while you're there? There are plenty of options—from historic hotels to campsites that you can only get to on foot. It just depends on how much you want to (or don't want to) rough it. The hotels look after just about everything for you and can set up any kind of tour you might want to take. If you prefer to camp, there are twelve campgrounds in the park with over two thousand campsites. That may sound like a lot, but camping is very popular in Yellowstone and the campsites fill up quickly.

Most people think of visiting the park in the

summertime, but Yellowstone is a great place to visit in the winter. However, you will need to be able to brave the cold. Temperatures range from zero to twenty degrees Fahrenheit during the day. And temperatures below zero are common, especially at night and at higher elevations.

You'll see Yellowstone in a different way in the winter. It truly becomes a land of fire and ice.

The landscapes become snowy winter wonderlands, and you'll see frosty and even snow-covered animals. The hot springs and geysers transform into magical sights in the cold temperatures. And you can take a tour of the park on snowshoes, in a snow truck, or on a snowmobile.

Of course, Yellowstone has lots to offer in the spring and fall as well. So, no matter what season you visit, you will not be disappointed!

Yellowstone Top Ten

There are so many things to see and do at Yellowstone National Park that it is hard to make a list of what not to miss. Here are some suggestions:

1. Watch the eruption of Old Faithful: Try and get to the viewing area early and get a good seat.

2. Spot wildlife in Lamar Valley: Keep your eyes open for bison, elk, wolves, and bears.

3. Go fishing at Yellowstone Lake: The lake is the largest high-elevation lake in North America.

4. Stroll the boardwalk at Grand Prismatic Spring: This is one of the world's largest hot springs. The layers of color in the water are unbelievable!

5. Explore Mammoth Hot Springs: This unique hydrothermal feature is a sight to behold.

6. Take a hike: There are over nine hundred miles of hiking trails in the park, such as Fairy Falls Trail and Mystic Falls Trail.

7. Go for a swim: It's a great way to cool off after a day of sightseeing.

8. Take in a waterfall: There are almost three hundred to choose from.

9. Snap some photos of the Roosevelt Arch: Built in 1903, the arch is at the North Entrance of the park. It was dedicated by President Theodore Roosevelt and contains a time capsule.

10. Explore the other Grand Canyon: The Grand Canyon in Yellowstone isn't as big as the Grand Canyon in Arizona, but it's just as breathtaking.

Roosevelt Arch

CHAPTER 8
The Future of Yellowstone

Around four million people visit Yellowstone National Park every year. And that number is sure to continue to rise since the park is more popular than ever. But with that many visitors each year, it is a challenge to keep the park in a natural state and allow it to be open and accessible to tourists.

Visitors are important to Yellowstone, but their presence can have negative effects on the park and its ecosystem. Visitors often want to get too

 close to the wildlife, which can cause the animals stress. They also walk off designated paths, trampling plants and destroying landforms.

Visitors also often leave

their trash behind. It pollutes the park, and unfortunately animals may eat it. And more visitors mean more vehicles, which adds to the air pollution, harms plants and animals, and also contributes to climate change.

What may not be obvious is that visitors in the park also change the soundscape, or natural sounds, in the park. The sound of all the vehicle traffic can make it difficult for animals to hear each other's calls, hear approaching prey, or hear mating calls. This can make it tough for the wildlife in the park to behave naturally—and for humans to enjoy the peace and quiet of the park.

Visitors should always follow the rules of the park and respect the special environment that is Yellowstone. And if possible, it's better to join a tour than to take your own vehicle into the park. Stay on the designated trails and boardwalks, and *never* remove any of the natural features. "Leave No Trace" is a good motto to follow. It means to make sure that things are left as you found them.

However, it isn't just tourism that can harm the park. Yellowstone is under threat from climate change. The earth is warming up, and in the past few decades, the warming planet has caused changes at the park. Scientists have recorded less snowpack, shorter winters, longer summers, and a bigger risk of wildfires. (Snowpack is the total amount of snow and ice on the ground that stays until the arrival of warm weather.)

The story of Yellowstone National Park is filled with highs and lows, triumphs and tragedies. But hopefully lessons have been learned and the park will continue to evolve. Yellowstone remains a symbol of how much the world needs to preserve and protect the wilderness. We need to make sure Yellowstone is here for hundreds of years to come.

The Fires of 1988

In 1988, Yellowstone National Park had a wet spring. But hardly any rain fell after June, which made it easy for fires to start in the park. By the middle of July, around 8,500 acres had burned in the park due to fires caused by lightning and human carelessness. That wasn't too unusual. But by the end of July, those fires were out of control and around 99,000 acres had burned.

On August 20, strong winds increased the size of the fires, and 150,000 acres burned just on that day. The day became known as "Black Saturday." The fires were not extinguished until snow fell in September. In total, 36 percent of the park, 793,000 acres, burned.

Many people thought the park was destroyed forever, but that wasn't the case. Even though the fires of 1988 changed the park's landscape, they didn't destroy it. Seedling trees appeared the following year. They are now healthy, strong, tall trees. The fires also created a "living laboratory" for scientists to learn how ecosystems like Yellowstone recover from severe fires.

The fires of 1988 were devastating. However, they proved that Yellowstone National Park and its ecosystem are strong. For the park to continue to thrive, we need to look after and protect it.

Timeline of Yellowstone

mya = million years ago

c. 30 mya	Most of the Yellowstone region's mountains are formed
c. 2.1 mya	First major volcanic eruption in the Yellowstone region
c. 11,000 years ago	Humans move into the Yellowstone region
1827	First written account of the Yellowstone region appears in a Philadelphia newspaper
1869	Folsom-Cook-Peterson Expedition of the region
1870	Washburn-Langford-Doane Expedition of the region
1871	Hayden Expedition to the region
1872	Yellowstone National Park is established
1915	Automobiles allowed in the park
1916	National Park Service is created
1948	Yellowstone National Park receives more than one million visitors
1970	Feeding of bears is prohibited
1988	Wildfires burn 793,000 acres
1995	Gray wolves reintroduced into the park
2021	Yellowstone welcomes 4.86 million visitors after park fully reopens following the COVID-19 pandemic
2022	Yellowstone National Park celebrates its 150th birthday

Timeline of the World

c. 65 mya	Dinosaurs become extinct
c. 11,500 years ago	The last Ice Age ends
c. 3100 BCE	Start of ancient Egyptian civilization
250– 900 CE	Height of the Mayan Empire
c. 570	Birth of the prophet Muhammad
1215	Magna Carta is signed in England
c. 1400	The Aztecs build their empire in Mexico
1620	The Pilgrims sail from England to North America on the Mayflower
1775	The American Revolution begins
1861	Start of the American Civil War
1920	Women given the right to vote in the United States
1945	World War II ends
1969	Neil Armstrong becomes the first person to walk on the moon
2007	Introduction of the iPhone
2012	Superstorm Sandy hits the East Coast of the United States
2020	Joe Biden is elected the forty-sixth president of the United States
2023	Wildfires devastate the island of Maui, Hawaii

Bibliography

*Books for young readers

Black, George. *Empire of Shadows: The Epic Story of Yellowstone*. New York: St. Martin's Press, 2012.

Chapple, Janet. *Yellowstone Treasure: The Traveler's Companion to the National Park*. Lake Forest Park, Washington: Granite Peak Publications, 2020.

Henry, Jeff. *Yellowstone National Park: The First 150 Years*. Lanham, Maryland: Lyons Press, 2022.

*Holland, Ilona E. *Buddy Bison's Yellowstone Adventure*. Washington, DC: National Geographic Kids, 2016.

*Johanek, Durrae. *What I Saw! in Yellowstone*. Helena, Montana: Riverbend Publishing, 2012.

Nelson, Megan Kate. *Saving Yellowstone: Exploration and Preservation in Reconstruction America*. New York: Scribner, 2022.

*Peabody, Erin. *A Weird and Wild Beauty: The Story of Yellowstone, the World's First National Park*. New York: Sky Pony Press, 2016.

Schullery, Paul. *Searching for Yellowstone: Ecology and Wonder in the Last Wilderness*. Boston: Houghton Mifflin, 1997.

Website

www.nps.gov/yell/index.htm (United States National Park Service, Yellowstone National Park)